GW00503262

DIDO

THE UNAUTHORISED BIOGRAPHY

IN WORDS AND PICTURES

COPYRIGHT © 2001 CHROME DREAMS.

FIRST PUBLISHED IN GREAT BRITAIN IN 2001 BY CHROME DREAMS.

ALL RIGHTS RESERVED. NO PART OF THIS BOOK MAY BE REPRODUCED IN ANY FORM OR BY ANY ELECTRONIC OR MECHANICAL MEANS, INCLUDING INFORMATION STORAGE OR RETRIEVAL SYSTEMS, NOR BE OTHERWISE CIRCULATED WITHOUT THE PUBLISHER'S PRIOR WRITTEN CONSENT IN ANY FORM OF BINDING OR COVER OTHER THAN THAT IN WHICH IT IS PUBLISHED.

A CATALOGUE RECORD FOR THIS BOOK IS AVAILABLE FROM THE BRITISH LIBRARY.

ISBN 184240 158 0

TEXT BY **SALLY WILFORD**
EDITED BY **BILLY DANCER**
ART DIRECTION AND DESIGN BY **A CREATIVE EXPERIENCE, LONDON**

PRINTED AND BOUND IN THE UK.

CHROME DREAMS
PO BOX 230
NEW MALDEN
SURREY KT3 6YY
UK

DIDO

THE UNAUTHORISED BIOGRAPHY

IN WORDS AND PICTURES

www.chromedreams.co.uk

CONTENTS

(I)
INTRODUCTION

Very rarely does an artist take the charts by storm on a global scale while also managing to attain that elusive goal of critical acclaim. Dido, however, has done both. Her outstandingly beautiful songs are imbued not only with supreme lyrical acuteness but also contain a succession of stunning vocal performances – a marriage not often witnessed in today's popular music charts. But Dido's music is not some esoteric artistic endeavour that satisfies the desires of a rarefied niche market. It's accessibility, directness and relevance has led to a widespread recognition of her talents across the globe, catapulting her into the dizzy realms of multi-platinum selling recording artist.

This level of achievement, though, has been far from easy to attain. From the many hours of musical practice that took her to one of the world's top music colleges, through the hard slog of touring as a jobbing backing vocalist to her elder brother's band, Dido's rise to fame and fortune has been long and eventful. Determined to make it as a solo artist with her own unique brand of soulful and electronic sounds, she faced yet another struggle to get her songs into the consciousness of true music lovers everywhere.

But it is the music itself that has made her so popular. Where the success of some other artists may be due to hype and the cult of 'personality', Dido has got where she is today through sheer unbridled musical talent. Apart from the sensuous lyrics, laid back trip-hop beats, scratching from live decks and melodic acoustic guitar riffs, her lush mellow vocals are the element that sets the whole combination apart. With a voice echoing Enya, Beth Orton and Sarah McLachlan, but at the same time superseding these influences, the unique sound of Dido is now firmly entrenched in our collective musical landscape. This is the story of how it happened.

CHAPTER 1
QUEEN OF ISLINGTON

1971 and it's Christmas Eve at a London hospital where a young couple are seriously beginning to doubt whether the festive season would ever be the same again. The contractions had begun during the night of December 24th, and a little over twenty-four painful hours later, a small screaming bundle was placed in the arms of its mother. The Armstrong family was now complete; mother Clare, father William and elder brother Roland could not have been happier. Quite literally, on Christmas Day of that year, a star was born.

Born to a homemaker mother and a literary agent father, the new arrival possessed a strength of character and fervour so formidable that her parents could think of only one name for her. That of one of Latin literature's strongest female characters - the great warrior Queen of Carthage; and so, Dido practically named herself. A strong name for a strong-willed little girl, with a zest for life so enormous, that anything she put her mind to, she succeeded in. Little wonder with the environment in which she was raised. This young girl of English-Irish descent, spent her formative years growing up in the comfortable surroundings of a small house in Islington. Whilst her father went out to work, her mother endeavoured to turn their home into a haven where creativity and art would flourish. As Dido and her brother, now forever nicknamed Rollo, watched their mum scribbling down numerous poems that she had composed each week, they too began to catch the bug to create. Denied access to a television, they had little choice but to produce their own entertainment, and started to display a flair and talent for imaginative pursuits. Even if one episode did involve Rollo pushing his little sister down a flight of stairs and then putting itching powder in her bed just to amuse himself, the siblings grew close and many of their activities were more productive.

Dido showed innovation when it came to occupying her time, and began hungering for different kinds of ways to pass the hours. As she turned five, she started to experience the initial stirrings of a passion to play a musical instrument but, much to her annoyance, her parents were not keen to buy her one. Fate stepped in, however, and one day she noticed a small brown and cream plastic tube in the lost and found at school. She couldn't believe her luck - it was a recorder which no one appeared to be claiming. Her yearning to own a musical instrument got the better of her and she took it. From that moment on, Dido was one hundred percent addicted to playing music.

Every day, she would rush home from school and wait for her parents to busy themselves somewhere else so she could play it in secret. And play it she did. From the age of five, she would practice for hours at a time getting carried away by the Bach concertos that her fingers and breath were producing. Eventually, her mother caught her, but upon witnessing her phenomenal ability, was not only amazed but now also extremely supportive of her young daughter's chosen path. And so, in 1978, Dido Armstrong and someone else's abandoned recorder, were accepted into the Guildhall School of Music in London.

Clare and William's little girl could not have been happier and as the years passed, her musical capabilities continued to strengthen and flourish. By the time she celebrated her tenth birthday, she was declared a child prodigy, having not only superbly mastered the recorder but also the piano and violin.

1985 was to be a very special year for Dido. She had managed to be accepted into a classical music ensemble that toured up and down the country, but more importantly, she also found herself attending an audition for a student opera at Westminster Abbey. It was here that she finally discovered her beautiful vocal abilities. Realising that she possessed an even more powerful musical instrument in her lungs, she decided to join the Abbey's choir and continued to sing there on a regular basis for the next few years. She was also in the midst of discovering something else though, and that something, was 'boys'.

Dido was now into the teenage years and with it arrived the endless fascination with clothes, make-up and the opposite sex. She still continued to tour with her classical ensemble up until she turned nineteen, but this style of music was no longer the number one priority in her life. Along with boys, she had fallen in love with the smoky jazz vocals of Ella Fitzgerald as well as more modern bands such as The Police. By the time she finished school in 1991, Dido had a very clear idea of what she wanted to do and, true to form, put all her effort into trying to achieve it.

Initially aiming to following in her father's footsteps, Dido was eventually granted entry into the world of words where she found employment as a literary agent. Such a routine nine-to-five existence, though, was not nearly enough to satisfy her creative impulses. And so, whilst she spent her daylight hours alternating between greasing the wheels of the publishing world and studying at law school, during the evenings she could be seen assuming an altogether very different guise: singing self-penned songs with a band backing her onstage. She had taken that first step on the ladder to making pop music.

CHAPTER 2
KING ROLLO

Whilst his younger sister had been adding as many strings to her bow as possible – singing, studying musical instruments and working as a literary agent to name but a few – Roland 'Rollo' Armstrong was also trying to find his niche. Experiences such as swimming the Ganges, winning the North-Yorkshire heats of the Disco Dancing Championship, working as a barman in Sydney and as a gardener for Islington council, had done little to help him decide which career path to pursue. At a loss as to which direction he wanted his life to head in, he took the plunge and enrolled at university. Three years later, he left with an honours degree in philosophy tucked under his belt but still felt unsatisfied.

Then one day in 1991, whilst Dido was storming the publishing world in between touring the club circuit, he found his calling. As he lazed in his bedroom chatting to two of his friends – Francis Wright and Red Jerry – the three of them decided to mess around on his mini recording studio. The result was a dance track called 'Don't You Want Me' and in January 1992, under the band name Felix, it managed to sell 2.2 million copies. Rollo had found where both his talent and passion lay, and just like his sister, it was within the arena of music.

As the years rolled by, the two siblings pursued their respective careers which went from strength to strength. Dido developed into a very successful literary agent and due to her considerable abilities in her chosen field, was now earning a very comfortable salary. Rollo continued to mix and produce tracks, but gradually decided that the time had come for him to form his own record label. As a result, in 1994, Rollo and his friend Mel Medalie pooled their resources and Cheeky Records was born. Although it may appear that the careers of the Armstrong siblings couldn't have been more different, unbeknown to them, their respective worlds were about to collide.

By the following year both had reached a turning point in their lives. Rollo had become phenomenally successful as a writer, producer and remixer for bands such as Pet Shop Boys, M People, Simply Red and Livin' Joy, but he also found himself desperately wanting to try something new. He was keen to collaborate with other musicians on a long-term project and set about finding like-minded individuals to form a band. Before long he managed to pull in the talents of Jamie Catto, Sister Bliss and Maxi Jazz and the four of them started co-writing and performing under the moniker of Faithless.

At the same time, Dido had also reached a watershed in her young life. She had met and fallen in love with a new boyfriend called Bob Page. This made her stand still and seriously take stock of where she was heading. Foremost in the whirlwind of thoughts and emotions that consumed her was the simple fact that music was too deeply engrained in her soul to be just an evening past-time. What she really wanted to do was record an album of the songs that she had been writing since she was nineteen. Dido now faced a dilemma. She knew her brother's band project Faithless would be the ideal place to start pursuing her dream, but she felt too afraid to ask Rollo for her big break.

As a result, whilst Faithless worked on their first album, Dido decided to hang around the studio on the off-chance that she might be asked to contribute her vocals to a song. After spending many hours waiting around and making endless cups of tea for the band, her persistence eventually paid off. Whilst laying down one particular track, Rollo decided that it really needed the input of a backing vocalist. Sister Bliss recommended that they should ask Dido, to which Rollo allegedly replied "my sister can't sing". But upon hearing her lovely voice properly for the first time, he became aware of just how misguided he'd been. The deal she'd wanted for so long was sealed at last: Dido Armstrong was signed to her brother's record label Cheeky and was now an official member of the trip-hop outfit Faithless. However, Rollo, ever the teasing older sibling, continued to take the view that she "shouldn't give up her day job".

But the band had now become everyone's day job and in September 1995, Faithless released their first single *Salva Mea*. It was moderately successful but did little to prepare them for the events of the following year. In summer 1996 their second offering, *Insomnia*, was released and they soon had a bona fide smash record on their hands – a track that not only became an international clubbing anthem, but also a top-ten world wide hit.

Although Dido had entered the year of 1996 as a mere twenty-four year old, she would see it out feeling a lot older and wiser. Apart from a hit single, within those twelve months, Faithless' debut album *Reverence* was also recorded, mixed and released. In addition to her backing vocals, the track 'Flowerstand Man' also featured a lead vocal from Dido as well as an opportunity for her to show her composing talents through co-writing it with Rollo.

Her life had become a whirlwind roller-coaster of both extremely uplifting and soul-destroying experiences. She had achieved the amazing feat of collaborating on an album that would eventually go on to sell a staggering five million copies, but at the same time had, paradoxically, secured a misery and loneliness that would envelop her for the next eighteen months. Eighteen months which would see her, Rollo and the rest of the band, touring the world and keep her away from the new found love of her life Bob Page. This separation would, though, prove ultimately to be a blessing in disguise. During this period, when she felt like the aching and longing would consume her completely, Dido began to work again on her own solo material. One recording session yielded a song called 'I'm No Angel'. Dido Armstrong was on her way.

In the midst of the ceaseless touring, every time Dido returned to London she found time to lay down tracks for her first demo tape. By the time 1997 had begun, the twenty-five-year-old future pop chanteuse had managed to assemble a whole album's worth of demos. This achievement in itself gave her a much needed confidence boost, and she was in one hundred percent agreement when her brother suggested that they start approaching record labels with a view to having it released. As it turned out, they didn't have to approach very many at all.

It so happened that Clive Davis – the president of the American branch of Arista Records - was in London. He had discovered and signed superstars such as Santana, Sarah McLachlan, Janis Joplin and Whitney Houston, and having got hold of Dido's demo tape, was eager to make contact with her. As a result, in early 1997, a nervous young woman entered the Dorchester Hotel in London for a meeting with this music industry legend – she needn't have worried though. Upon hearing her sing a couple of her self-penned songs, Davis signed her on the spot and Dido Armstrong became the first direct signing to Arista USA in over ten years.

Everything in her life was now focused solely on preparing for and completing her first album. By now, Dido had moved out of the family home and was living with her brother in London. When he offered to help produce and mix the record with his partner Youth, it seemed the perfect set-up. Despite this, Dido was keen to have as much control as possible

over her work and decided that she would have the final say on matters of production. Rollo and Youth were happy with this arrangement. and so in the summer of 1997 all three entered the studio to lay down the initial tracks. Writing and producing the album was second nature to Dido, and securing a record deal had been pretty plain sailing, but getting the music out to the public was another matter entirely.

Dido's lush vocals, ethereal acoustics and electronic sounds and loops, were so unique that Arista were unclear as to how to promote and publicise their new found gem. Once Dido had produced a number of finished tracks, they decided to test the waters by releasing them on a promotional EP called *Highbury Fields*. A limited number of these were pressed and resulted in a small underground following for Dido amongst college students in the USA who had heard the record played on their student radio stations.

Despite this, as 1998 began, such good news was doing little to raise Dido's spirits. Her boyfriend Bob was away from her but, as always, she tried to channel the associated negative emotions into creativity. By the end of January she had managed to compose three new songs for the album: 'All You Want', 'Don't Think Of Me' and 'Hunter'. In addition to working on her own record, Dido was also busy with Faithless' new release *Sunday 8pm*, contributing two tracks entitled 'Postcards' and 'Hem Of His Garment'. She was clearly eager to gain as much exposure for her music as possible and so the next offer she received was simply too irresistible to refuse.

Upon being asked if she'd like to contribute one of her songs, 'Thank You', to the soundtrack of an up-and-coming low-budget British film, she had no problem saying yes. Although she didn't know it at the time, it was a decision that would drastically alter the course of her life. The movie she was contributing to was called *Sliding Doors* and featured the famous Hollywood actress Gwyneth Paltrow. This film was not only a box-office smash that boosted the profile of Dido and her music amongst cinema-goers, it happened to attract the attention of one viewer in particular. His name was Marshall Mathers. Things were about to get even more hectic in the world of Dido Armstrong.

Faithless (Rollo Armstrong Second From Right)

CHAPTER 4
WOMAN ON THE VERGE

Although the amount of money spent on an artist by its record label is by no way indicative of the quality of the music, the fact that Arista invested about half-a-million dollars in Dido's first video, more than adequately demonstrated their faith and belief in her talent and musical capabilities. Such was their confidence in her future success, that they drafted in Academy, the team responsible for ground-breaking music videos from George Michael, Mary J. Blige and Lauryn Hill. And so, in early 1999, Dido released her first solo single, the haunting and delicate ode to love, *Here With Me* and its accompanying glossy video.

This latter promotional tool gradually began to be screened on the television music channels MTV2 and The Box, but much to Arista and Dido's dismay, it never broke into the mainstream. More popular channels such as VH1 or MTV were reluctant to include the video in their schedules while radio play of the track ranged from infrequent to non-existent.

Unfortunately, everyone had to face the truth. The worst-case scenario had actually transpired - Dido Armstrong had bombed. Although this is traditionally the stage at which many fledgling music careers are ended, no one at Arista was ready to give up on Dido yet. There had to be some way of making the masses aware of such gorgeous and melancholic music.

With Dido's solo album ready to be released, the executives at Arista decided that they need to build upon the small US following that had been garnered through the issue of the *Highbury Fields EP*. In addition to constantly plugging the album to radio stations and passing copies to music journalists, they decided that Dido should embark on a promotional tour of the USA. As a result, in May 1999 Dido hit the road playing at in-store appearances and small venues – often performing in front of as little as thirty people. Progress was slow but a fan-base of sorts was beginning to appear. The day of reckoning soon arrived and on the first of June, after two years in the making, Dido's debut album *No Angel* was finally released.

Much to everyone's relief, it received rave reviews wherever it was mentioned. The critics were unanimous in their opinions – Dido Armstrong's debut release was a masterpiece. The twelve tracks, knitted together and unified by sweeping orchestral arrangements, gorgeous acoustic guitars and vocal harmonies, possessed a unique fragility. The consensus view was that she had broken new barriers in releasing an album with catchy sing-along choruses, beautiful melodies, and a warm, full-bodied sound that sensitively mixed both traditional and electronic instruments. In their eyes, she could do no wrong but unfortunately, whilst she may have received huge amounts of critical appreciation, attention from the record buying public failed to materialise.

Despite this, several developments transpired to save Dido from musical oblivion. Firstly, in July, months after its release, *Here With Me* was chosen as the theme song for the teen cult series *Roswell*. Secondly, during the last week of July, she performed on the prestigious Lilith Fair outdoor festival tour – gigs which guaranteed her appearance in front of large audiences. At last she'd got her break; such national exposure meant that by the end of the month, *Here With Me* had finally moved into the top forty of the US radio play list.

Dido was clearly on her way and she hastily began laying the groundwork for a major headlining tour of North America. This started in August with an initial show in Vancouver, winding up in Boston at the start of October. Flushed with her success, Dido had no intention of putting on the brakes and losing the momentum she had built up. She therefore spent the last month of the old millennium on another mini-tour of the US. The resulting television appearance on David Letterman's *The Late Show* truly signalled that Dido was going places.

After a brief rest in January, Dido kicked off the year 2000 with some dates in New York to coincide with the radio release of the single *Don't Think Of Me*. In addition, after a slow climb of more than ten months, *No Angel* had reached the number four spot on the radio album chart. A performance on the *Conan O'Brien Show* in March concluded the tour in a blaze of glory. But nothing could prepare her for what happened next.

CHAPTER 5
ANGEL IN DISGUISE

Some months previously, Dido had been sent a track for approval, which had sampled her sweet, light tune 'Thank You' into a dark tale about an obsessive fan who sends a degenerative series of unanswered letters to his idol. She had given the go-ahead for the artist to use a sample of this song on his new album. That album was called *The Marshall Mathers LP*, the track was entitled 'Stan' and it was by the world's best-selling rap artist Eminem.

And so, in May of 2000, Dido's sweet and dulcet tones could be heard on an album other than her own. This 'other' album, however, just happened to debut at number one on the Billboard Album Chart and also generated the second biggest first-week sales figures in the history of the record business. She had last been given her big break.

In the same week that Eminem's new release debuted, *No Angel* made a sudden return to the Billboard Top Two-Hundred Chart, re-entering at number one-hundred-and-forty-four. Encouraged by the fact that her music was now starting to catch the attention of the wider record buying public, Dido hit the road once more. The tour began in Albany, finishing two months later on the 15th of July with a final show in Las Vegas. Her public profile was further advanced when

Sarah Brightman, the British opera singer and ex-wife of the hugely successful composer Andrew Lloyd Webber, released a cover version of 'Here With Me'. At the same time, the band Dusted - consisting of Dido's brother Rollo and his friend Mark Bates working under a pseudonym – released their debut album *While We Were Young*. In the midst of all her success, Dido had even found time to co-write three of the tracks on this release – 'Always Remember To Respect and Honour Your Mother (Part One)', 'The Biggest Fool In The World' and 'Winter'. With a rising awareness of and growing adulation for her music, Dido was keen to get back on the road as soon as possible. This time it was a little different though – in August Dido embarked on her own headlining tour.

This tour started with some great news for Dido. *No Angel* had now broken into the top one-hundred of the Billboard Chart. To back up the album, a new version of the single *Here With Me* was released with a new video to accompany it. By early September, the video was receiving heavy rotation on MTV2, however, there was an even more exciting prospect just around the corner. Eminem's record company had decided to release 'Stan' as the next single from *The Marshall Mathers LP*. Eminem requested that Dido appear in the video in person. Without a moment's hesitation she jumped at the chance.

With the video for 'Stan' receiving equal amounts of MTV airplay and media criticism for the controversial subject matter, the song 'Here With Me' appeared on the soundtrack to another Gwyneth Paltrow movie called *Bounce* in which she co-starred with Ben Affleck. To pick up on some of the new found interest in Dido's music, Arista also finally released her album in Europe. With a show-stopping appearance on *Saturday Night Live* to perform 'Stan' along with Eminem, it appeared life couldn't get any better. But the next few weeks would prove that observation wrong. As the year closed, and her brother celebrated his record label Cheeky being sold to BMG Records for a very large sum of money indeed, Dido toasted her own most recent phenomenal achievement. On Christmas Day, as she raised her glass to celebrate her 29th birthday, Dido had received her best combined birthday and Christmas present ever. *Stan* was the Christmas number one single in the UK.

CHAPTER 6
MUSIC TO FLOAT ON

Dido's decision to allow Eminem to sample a portion of one of her songs, finally gave her the boost that she so desperately needed. The problem had never been the music – all along that had been well crafted and accessible. The difficulty had always been in how to find a way of marketing Dido to the record buying public, especially as her music can not be easily pigeon-holed into one particular style or genre. The appearance of a classically trained singer, like Dido, on a track produced by the rap legend Dr Dre might have seemed ludicrous, but with hindsight it was actually the contribution of her distinctive voice and lyrics that had made the song particularly effective. The surprisingly thoughtful exchange between Eminem and the psychotic fan only worked so well because the looped sample from *Thank You* soared above the spoken words. Her vocals had given the song the edge it needed and ensured its phenomenal popularity all over the world. After debuting in the top five of the singles charts in several countries, *Stan* had turned out to be so much more than a runaway success; it had finally opened the door for Dido, and provided her with instant exposure to a huge audience. Furthermore, Eminem's insistence that she join him on stage for a few of the concerts on his Anger Management Tour, also allowed fans of a different genre of music entirely, to experience a taste of her material live. Her fanbase was now expanding at an incredible rate.

Four days into the new year, Dido received the wonderful news that *No Angel* was at number seventeen on the Billboard Album Chart. Due to the success of her collaboration with Eminem, *Thank You* debuted at number eighty on the Billboard Top One-Hundred Singles Chart. It was even chosen to be featured in the background of a love scene involving the Hollywood star Sharon Stone, on the extremely popular prime time American television series *If These Walls Could Talk*.

The interest that Dido was generating in the USA was now huge. This interest was matched by an increase in sales of her debut album which finally broke into the top ten of the Billboard Chart on the 11th of January. Arista now decided that this popularity in the USA, combined with the massive sales in Europe, where *No Angel* had been storming up the charts, more than warranted a release in her native country. In addition, it was also decided that she would embark on a European tour later in the year. Performing live had always been what Dido loved doing best, but it also gave her a rare opportunity to give something back to her long-standing European fans for their unwavering loyalty and support. However, she was also eager to find a different method of showing her appreciation – something that was a little bit extra special. And so, at her instigation, Dido's record company began to get in contact with the individual creators of the multitude of websites dedicated to discussing her and her music that had suddenly sprung up within the internet community over the last few months. It was decided that every couple of weeks, Jared Willig, from the label's marketing department, would email these websites with exclusive news about developments within the Dido camp and also send the webmasters promotional CD's and autographed merchandise to give to the fans as competition prizes. Such a move not only gave lovers of her music a taste of things to come, but also truly demonstrated just how much Dido wanted to acknowledge their support and faith in her work.

By mid-January, her music had made such a strong impact on the record buying public, that her debut album was climbing the UK charts and had reached number eleven – a great feat in itself, but even more remarkable, because it had broken the top twenty before she had even released her first commercial single there. Encouraged by such an amazing achievement, it was decided that more dates should be added to the UK leg of the tour. The video to her recent US single *Thank You* was also released and quickly received heavy rotation on both VH1 and MTV. Above all, the real significance of this lay in the fact that it truly symbolised just how famous Dido and her music had become; so famous, in fact, that her album *No Angel* had just been certified platinum. January ended in the way it had begun – Dido was still conquering the heights of international stardom with an album at number eight on the Billboard Album Charts, a single at number forty-seven on the Billboard Top One-Hundred single charts, and a music video that was in the top ten of both the MTV and VH1 promo charts.

Nothing, though, prepared her for the buzz that she felt at the beginning of the following month. After hitting it big in the States as a result of her duet with Eminem, she had come home to conquer her own country in the flesh, and conquer it she did. On the 7th of February, accompanied by the New York based band that she had now been touring with for two years, she performed a London gig at The Scala – the concert just happened to have been sold out for weeks.

A few days later, Dido made another appearance at a sold out venue, but this time, it had nothing whatsoever to do with her own tour. At a London Arena show, thousands of fans at an Eminem gig were surprised and delighted when he brought Dido onto the stage to perform their number one international smash hit *Stan*. There was only one way to finish such a fantastic month – the time had come for Dido Armstrong to release her first single *Here With Me* in her native country.

CHAPTER 7
SIREN OF SONG

Dido now had the perfect opportunity to show her fellow country men and women exactly what she was made of. Releasing *Here With Me* seemed a great way to achieve this, being one of the most beautiful and accessible tracks off the album. With a lilting lullaby chorus, huge Massive Attack–esque strings, chunky dance beats and touching lyrics about the heartache of missing a loved one, it is Dido at her best. It had already wafted around within the consciousness of the British public due to the popular US television series *Roswell*. The first season of this programme had began showing in the UK some months earlier under the altered name of *Roswell High*. Within a few weeks of its airing, the BBC had been flooded with enquiries from viewers asking who sang the theme song and how they could get hold of it. Well, Dido was about to provide the answers to both of these questions. The single was finally made available to the British record buyer on the 12th February 2001. Early purchasers at the HMV store in London's Oxford Street managed to catch not only a personal signing session by Dido herself, but also live performances of 'All You Want', 'Here With Me' and 'Thank You'.

Dido Armstrong and her melodic, fragile music were now everywhere. Even to the point that Sir Elton John sang the sampled parts of her single *Thank You*

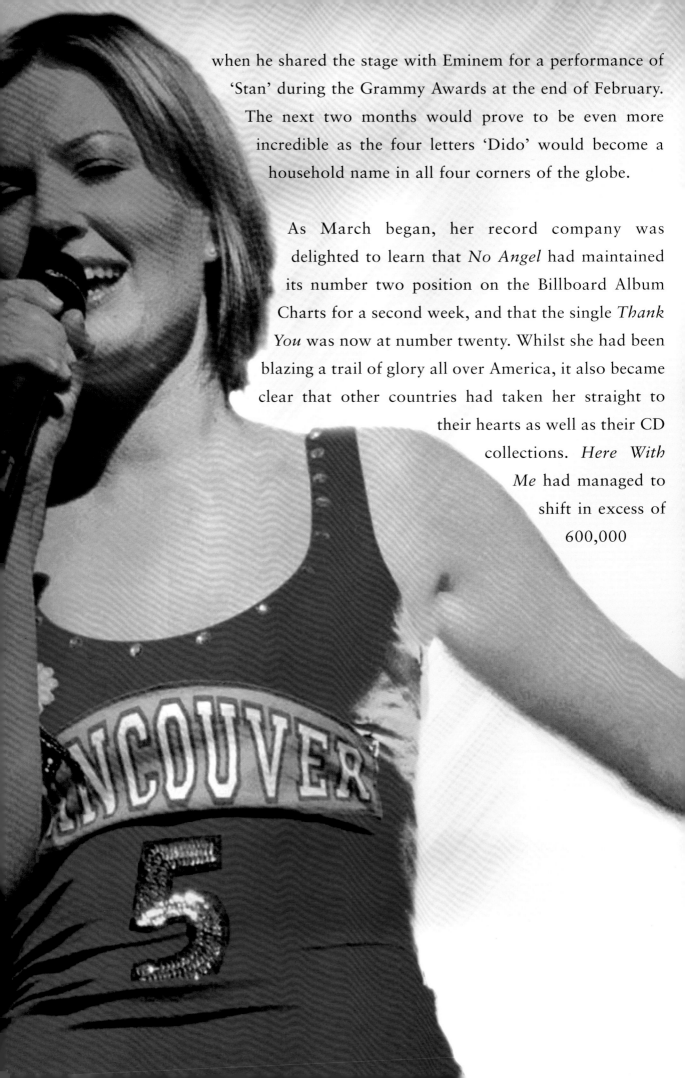

when he shared the stage with Eminem for a performance of 'Stan' during the Grammy Awards at the end of February. The next two months would prove to be even more incredible as the four letters 'Dido' would become a household name in all four corners of the globe.

As March began, her record company was delighted to learn that *No Angel* had maintained its number two position on the Billboard Album Charts for a second week, and that the single *Thank You* was now at number twenty. Whilst she had been blazing a trail of glory all over America, it also became clear that other countries had taken her straight to their hearts as well as their CD collections. *Here With Me* had managed to shift in excess of 600,000 units in the UK, her album was number two in Germany, and in New Zealand, not only was *No Angel* topping the charts with a platinum certification but 'Thank You' was the most played song on the radio. The best news was yet to come though.

On the 13th of March 2001, Dido Armstrong's ultimate dream came true: her debut album climbed to the number one position in the UK album charts. In addition, she was informed that it had now been certified triple-platinum. In Australia too, her musical popularity was still continuing to soar and, incredibly, she managed to repeat the same achievement she'd scored in the UK - *No Angel* had climbed to the top position even without the prior release of a single. Dido had every reason to just relax and bask in the glow of such an amazing success story but, as always, she was keen to get back to what she loved doing best – making music.

After an invitation from her elder brother Rollo and the other members of Faithless, she returned to the studio to help record some tracks for their new album *Outrospective*. Although visually out of the public arena, audibly she was never far from it. Yet another Dido track 'My Life' was now scheduled to feature in a new Jennifer Lopez movie called *Angel Eyes*. It was also announced that Dido would be taking her music on the road in the not too distant future, and that Travis – the musicians behind the multi-platinum selling album *The Man Who* - would be supporting her. The month of March may have ended with Rollo's baby sister being firmly ensconced in a recording studio, but it also ended with her happily occupying the number six position on the American charts with *Thank You*.

The next few weeks proved to be just as exciting as even more reasons to celebrate materialised. An online report by the BBC revealed that *No Angel* had sold three-million units in the USA and in excess of seven hundred thousand in the UK. Furthermore, her single *Here With Me* had managed to remain in the British charts for seven weeks running. Everything was now fantastic in the world of Dido

CHAPTER 8
SUCCESS COMES TO THOSE WHO WAIT

Six years earlier at a night-club, Dido's boyfriend at the time had introduced her to the most amazing man she had ever met: he was a lawyer and his name was Robert Page. The impact he made on her was so huge, that the next day she felt compelled to compose a new song and that song just happened to be the beautiful ballad 'Here With Me'. In April 2001, Bob got down on one knee and proposed marriage to his beautiful, multi-platinum album selling British girlfriend. Dido (not unsurprisingly given her feelings for him) immediately, wholeheartedly and happily accepted. As fate would have it though, the engagement celebrations were short-lived as, the very next day, she and her suitcase travelled away for the foreseeable future – it was time for the public to witness her musical talent and capabilities first-hand again.

On the 6th of April, Dido kicked off her international tour at the Glasgow Barrowlands; it was a tour that would keep her on the road for just over three months as she performed to sell-out audiences in Germany, France, Spain, Sweden, Belgium, Canada and North America. However, during those three months she not only dominated the gig circuits of Europe and America, but also continued to command a huge share of the world's radio airwaves, music charts and television channels.

It was revealed that Dido had written two songs for US pop sensation Britney Spears and that she was also going to team up with the nineteen-year-old to help produce several tracks, as well as pen new material for her forthcoming album. Dido's own solo work though, was still making huge waves within the music industry on a global scale: by mid-April *Here With Me* was number nineteen on the German charts and number thirty-three in the UK charts, whilst *Thank You* had climbed to number four in the U.S. More excitingly though, *No Angel* still had a firm grip within the top five of the UK charts and it was now decided that Dido's phenomenally successful debut album would be released in Japan. Such a decision seemed very wise as, by the end of April, the very same record was inhabiting the top ten of the charts in the US, the UK, Germany and Australia.

Dido saw in the first week of May 2001, by playing to sell out crowds in Stockholm, Oslo, Copenhagen, Hamburg and Brussels. Her pace of life was hectic to say the least, but the zest and sheer enthusiasm that she had displayed as a young child when she had religiously practiced the recorder every day after school, was still very much in evidence. In between a gruelling and exhausting tour schedule, she still managed to find the time to do interviews and photo-shoots, appearing most prestigiously on the cover of the best-selling American music magazine *Rolling Stone* with her gigging support act Travis. She also guested on the song 'One Step Too Far' – a track featured on the newly released Faithless album, *Outrospective*.

Much to her delight, she was also receiving praise in the media not only for her music, but also for her decision to allow the song 'Take My Hand' to be featured during a controversial kiss between Jack and Tobey in an episode of the hugely popular teen series *Dawson's Creek*. Both the gay and straight communities applauded such a move. In addition, along with the pop band Hear'Say, she was commended by the British Music Industry for substantially boosting the value of British record sales in the first financial quarter of 2001 – a time during which the combined sale of CD albums exceeded the one-billion pound mark for the first time. The fact that on the day the BMI announced this, Dido's album *No Angel* was enjoying its thirty-first week on the UK charts, seemed to further substantiate their claims. The album was not only number three on the UK album charts, selling, by that time over eight-million copies world-wide, but her new single *Thank You*, had also taken the single charts by storm, entering at number three.

By the beginning of June, Dido was celebrating the fact that *No Angel* had sold nearly three-million copies in the US. For the rest of June and the early part of July, she launched a head-lining tour of the US and Canada that would take her to sell out audiences all over North America. When these dates were completed on the 8th of July, Dido discovered that one of her wildest dreams was about to come true - she was to be the opening act for one of her childhood musical idols. Sting himself had requested that she be asked to support him for two sell-out gigs in Los Angeles. She had certainly come a long way from being a starry-eyed teenager who used to worship the posters of him tacked to her bedroom walls – now she was actually going to perform alongside him. Life didn't get any better than this.

CHAPTER 9
NO ANGEL, JUST A STAR

Dreamy pop is one way to describe Dido's music. Or electronica shadings married to folk guitars and soulful vocals that, when blended together, despite the denial in the title of her debut album, produces a kind of music that is one-hundred percent heavenly. Peppered with songs that are both sweet and soothing and anchored by formidable hypnotic beats, these are tunes that will never float away.

Dido's classical training has provided a musical grounding which appears to lend her songs a weight and indefinable logic that sounds just right. Maybe it's her English-Irish heritage that enables her to make music with such a tight hold on the past, and yet combined with a feel that is so completely contemporary it can't be readily placed. Whatever the reason, one thing is clear: her music stays with you like a dream you can't shake off.

Her gorgeous melancholic, lilting voice and extraordinary flowing, witty and charming lyrics have made a huge impact on anyone who has had the pleasure of hearing them. This accomplishment has resulted in her not only bewitching the critics, but also the public, and her music still continues to take the charts by storm all over the world. Through her talent, sheer determination and unwavering commitment to succeeding, Dido even managed to permeate the musical consciousness of America – an achievement attained by very few British music artists during their creative lifetime. Naturally enough, it has been a success that she has managed to repeat in her home country and upon hearing her songs, the UK public were just as quick to take Dido and her music to their hearts. Such international domination can mean one thing alone: clearly, this is a career that can only continue to go one way, and that way is up.

It is truly ironic then, that it was her own elder brother, Roland 'Rollo' Armstrong, who tried to dissuade her from pursuing a music career. It is to the record buying public's benefit though, that she chose to ignore him and instead share the sweet simplicity of her melodies and the complexity of her words with audiences all over the world. Such a decision has ensured that in Dido Armstrong, the music industry has one of its brightest stars. It is a star that will continue to sparkle with promise for a very long time to come. Of that we can be sure.

CHAPTER 9
DIDO QUOTES

"I'm an all right musician who is rubbish at everything. I used to be a great classical player but I let that slip. Sometimes I play piano live but then I can't sing. It's like rubbing your stomach and head at the same time."

"It knocks me down, the thought of being featured in the most popular video of the year and looking so dreadful."
Dido on the video For 'Stan'

"It's much better when I go out with my mates and we stop talking about me like I'm some sort of egomaniac. It's great when we can just have a drink."

"Everyone perceives him as a homophobe and misogynist whereas in fact he's a really nice guy"
Dido on Eminem

"I'd sit in the hotel room thinking "There will be the day that I'll show you who is the real vocalist here.""
Dido on touring with Faithless

"I can't go to Tesco without people following me down the aisles whispering, "That's her". It started off in Marks & Spencer's and now it's every supermarket."

"He's my greatest support. I travel and tour a lot, but I always know that afterwards I can go back to our London flat and he will be there waiting for me. It would be much harder for me if it weren't for his love and utmost patience."
Dido on her fiancé Bob

"When I heard 'Here With Me' on the radio for the first time, I thought it was actually playing from my CD player. When I realised it's the radio I phoned my brother straight away screaming "Can you hear it?! Can you hear it?! Do you know what it is?!" I was jumping with excitement all the time."

"I got really pissed off at the way they censored the Stan video. I've got a feeling that by some mysterious reason they cut off all these bits that truly warned: 'don't do it!' Because of this the video carries the opposite message to the one intended and can be easily misunderstood."

"I absolutely love it. You appear on TV with your new hairstyle and a week after you go out on the street you see girls with their hair cut just like yours."

"If someone takes an unfinished demo from the studio and puts it up on the Internet, I'll kill them."

"I go shopping, clean the flat, cook my boyfriend's dinner. It's great selling records, but it doesn't mean you have to turn into a freak."

"It doesn't matter how big the audience is, as long as they are enjoying it, it's fine. Watching Elton John singing my song with Eminem on the Grammys was just bizarre."

"I prefer writing songs to talking about them. There's more to life than doing interviews."

"I'm not actually putting me out through my lyrics. I'm trying to put feelings out. I'm not sort of saying this is me, because if I was, I'd be a psycho."

"I really love bananas but I'm worried the potassium will poison me."

CHAPTER 10
DISCOGRAPHY

SOLO ALBUMS

Highbury Fields EP
Here With Me / Hunter / My Lover's Gone / Honestly OK / Worthless – Five song promotional EP to promote Dido's 'No Angel' album. Released to record stores and radio stations only.
CD – Arista Records 1999

No Angel (US Version)
Here With Me / Hunter / Don't Think of Me / My Lover's Gone / All You Want / Thank You / Honestly OK / Slide / Isobel / I'm No Angel / My Life / Take My Hand
CD – Arista Records 1999

No Angel (US Promo with DVD Single)
Here With Me / Hunter / Don't Think of Me / My Lover's Gone / All You Want / Thank You / Honestly OK / Slide / Isobel / I'm No Angel / My Life / Take My Hand – Also contains a 'DVD' single with the videos for *Here With Me* and *Thank You* plus a photo gallery.
CD – Arista Records 1999

No Angel (Limited Edition Enhanced CD)
Here With Me / Hunter / Don't Think of Me / My Lover's Gone / All You Want / Thank You / Honestly OK / Slide / Isobel / I'm No Angel / My Life / Take My Hand – Also contains a second CD with the videos for *Here With Me* and *Thank You* plus a photo gallery.
CD - Arista Records 2001

No Angel (UK Release)
Here With Me / Hunter / Don't Think of Me / My Lover's Gone / All You Want / Thank You / Honestly OK / Slide / Isobel / I'm No Angel / My Life / Take My Hand
CD - Arista Records 2001

No Angel
Here With Me / Hunter / Don't Think Of Me / My Lover's Gone / All You Want / Thank You / Honestly OK / Slide / Isobel / I'm No Angel / My Life / Take My Hand – Also includes the two bonus tracks *Worthless* and *Me*.
CD – Arista Records 2001

SOLO SINGLES

Here With Me (US Promo)
Here With Me (Radio Edit) / Call Out Research Hook
CD – Arista Records 1999

Here With Me (US Promo):
Here With Me *(Rollo's Chillin' With The Family Mix)*
CD – Arista Records 1999

Here With Me (US Promo)
Here With Me (Radio Edit) / Here With Me (Lukas Burton Remix) / Here With Me (Call Out Research Hook)
CD – Arista Records 1999

Here With Me (UK Release)
Here With Me (Radio Edit) / Here With Me (Lukas Burton Mix) / Here With Me (Rollo's Chillin' With The Family Mix) / Here With Me (Parks & Wilson Homeyard Dub)
CD - Arista Records 2001

Here With Me
Here With Me (Radio Edit) / Here With Me (Lukas Burton Mix) / Here With Me (Chillin' With The Family Mix) / Here With Me (Parks & Wilson Homeyard Dub) / Thank You (Deep Dish Dub)
CD - Arista Records 2001

Here With Me (UK Promo)

Here With Me (Radio Edit)

CD - Arista Records 2001

Here With Me (UK 12" Promo)

Here With Me (Parks & Wilson´s Twilo Vocal) /
Here With Me (Parks & Wilson´s Homeyard Dub)

Vinyl - Arista Records 2001

Thank You (US Promo)

Thank You / Call Out Research Hook

CD - Arista Records 1999

Thank You (EU Single Release)

Thank You (Album Version) / Thank You (Deep Dish
Vocal) / Thank You (Skinny Mix) / Thank You
(Enhanced Video Version)

Enhanced CD - Arista Records 2000

Don't Think Of Me (US Promo)

Don't Think Of Me (Radio Mix) / Don't Think Of
Me (Album Version Edit) / Call Out Research Hook

CD - Arista Records 2000

Hunter (US Promo Release)

Hunter / Suggested Call-Out Research Hook

CD - 2001 Arista Records

Take My Hand (UK 12" Promo)

Dido´s Side: Take My Hand (Parks & Wilson´s Vocal
Mix) / Rachel´s Side: (Parks & Wilson Mix)

Vinyl - Arista Records 2001

SINGLE RELEASES WITH OTHER ARTISTS

Bad Man

Bad Man (7" Edit) / Bad Man (Original Mix) / Bad
Man (Epic Mix) / Bad Man (Junkdog Mix) - Dido
sings backing vocals on this release by Faithless
member Sister Bliss.

CD and Vinyl - Cheeky 1999

Failure:

Failure (Radio Mix)/ Failure (David Holmes Mix) /
Failure (Original Instrumental) / Failure (Magitone
Mix) – Skinny with Dido on backing vocals.

CD and Vinyl - Cheeky 1999

Stan (UK Promo Release)

Stan (Radio Version) / Stan (Album Version) /
Stan (Instrumental) - Eminem featuring Dido.

CD - Interscope Records 2000

Stan (Australian release)

Stan (Radio Edit) / Stan (Director´s Cut CD-Rom
Video) - Eminem Featuring Dido.

CD - Interscope Records 2000

ALBUM RELEASES WITH OTHER ARTISTS

Reverence

Flowerstand Man – Faithless featuring Dido who also sings backing vocals on six other tracks. Album reissued with additional track *Flowerstand Man (Matty's Remix).*

CD - Cheeky Records 1997

Sunday 8pm

Postcards / Hem Of His Garment - Faithless Featuring Dido. Also released with a second CD containing *Postcards (Rewritten Remix).*

CD – Cheeky Records 1999

The Marshall Mathers LP

Stan Eminem featuring Dido

CD – Interscope Records 2000

When We Were Young

Always Remember To Respect Your Mother Part 1 / The Biggest Fool In The World / Winter - Dido is credited as co-writer on these three songs.

CD - Polydor 2001

Outrospective

One Step Too Far - Faithless Featuring Dido.

CD – Arista 2001

COMPILATIONS

Lilith Fair Emerging Artists Sampler

Thank You

CD - EMM 1998

Pointfolio 1.0

Here With Me – This compilation of live performances was released by The Point radio station in Minneapolis. This acoustic version was recorded live in the Point Studios on the 25th of August 1999.

CD - The Point 1999

Live From The Mix Lounge

Here With Me

CD – Mix 98.5 1999

Various Artists Platinum Christmas

Christmas Day

CD - Jive Records 2000

Christmas Songs – The Netwerk Christmas

Christmas Day

CD – Nettwerk Records 2000

Totally Hits 3

Here With Me

CD – Arista Records 2000

This Is Alice Music: Volume 4

Thank You

CD – Alice @ 97.3 2000

Back To Mine

My Life – Chill-out album mixed by Rollo and Sister Bliss.

CD – DMC 2000

Brits 2001 Album Of The Year

Here With Me

CD – Sony 2001

Café Del Mar Volumen Ocho

Worthless

CD - Universal MCA 2001

Ministry Of Sound - The Chill Out Sessions Volume 2

Here With Me (Radio Edit)

CD - Ministry Of Sound 2001

Ray's House

Here With You (Parks And Wilson Homeyard Dub)

CD - BMG 2001

SOUNDTRACKS

Sliding Doors Motion Picture Soundtrack

Thank You

CD – Universal / MCA 1998

Bounce – Music From And Inspired By The Film Bounce

Here With Me

CD – Arista 2000

BOOKS

Dido: The Unauthorised Biography In Words And Pictures
Chrome Dreams 2001

VIDEOS

Here With Me (US DVD Release)
Here With Me (Video) / Thank You (Live)
DVD - 2001 Arista Records

WEBSITES

For sourcing additional information about Dido, you really can't beat the World Wide Web. There are numerous sites about Dido containing a wide range of biographical information, pictures, up-to-the-minute news and tour dates as well as MP3's of both her well known and rarer tracks. The following sites are among the most comprehensive and a good place to start finding out about Dido online. Search engines such as Yahoo and Google can uncover many more fan sites. Up-to-date information can also be found on general music sites such as www. rollingstone.com, www.nme.com, www.mtv.com and www.getmusic.com.

www.didomusic.com

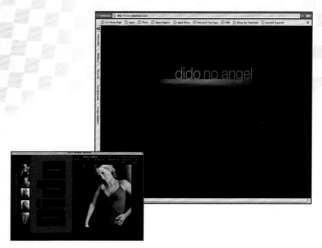

At this official record company site you can browse a short biography of Dido and view a photo gallery with five studio shots of the woman herself. There is also an audio and video section where you can listen to and watch several of Dido's most popular tracks. This site also includes a special news section where you can read all about what she is currently up to and contains a link to the Dido fan club which you can join on line. Overall this flashy site is currently not as full on content as the unofficial sites, but has some great photos and is still worth a look.

www.werkshop.com

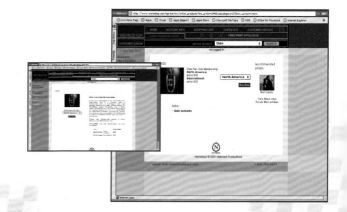

You can join the official Dido fan club online at this site. For your money you get a welcome letter, a membership card and three newsletters. There are also special exclusive ticketing offers for members as well as the promise of a limited edition fan club CD. Simply go to this site and follow the links to Dido.

www.faithlessangel.com

Great unofficial site – currently more content and better design than the official site! Run by Dido fan Robbie McCown, who has done stirling work, it includes a biography, news section and discography as well as a photo gallery with tons of cool shots and tour information. There is also a comprehensive links section and a guest book for users to leave comments about the site.

www.geocities.com/didohunter

This site called "Deep In My Own World" has a discography, the standard record company biography, a comprehensive collection of photos and a good links section. Lilly, who runs this site, has also included some Dido 'wallpaper' files that you can download to brighten up the desktop on your PC. There are also some lyrics as well as a guest book that users can sign.

http://clubs.yahoo.com/clubs/dido

This unofficial club site at Yahoo is a great way to get in touch with other Dido fans. Simply sign up free and you will be chatting to other Dido fans on-line in real time. You can also check back through messages that have been left in the past. There is also a members only photo section, a full list of other fans who have signed up and a Dido calendar.

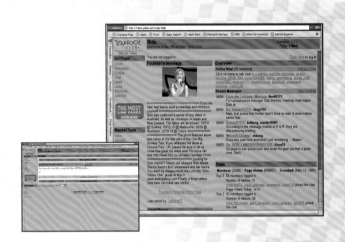

More Dido On The Web

Other sites that are well worth a look are:

http://blue-orange.org/dido/ - (**Dido message board**)

http://tydo.blue-orange.org

http://website.lineone.net/~alldido/

www.didozone.com

PHOTO CREDITS

Photos Courtesy of:

Redferns London
Famous Pictures London
Rex Features London

Also Available From Chrome Dreams:

Maximum Dido

The first ever Dido CD Audio-Biography.

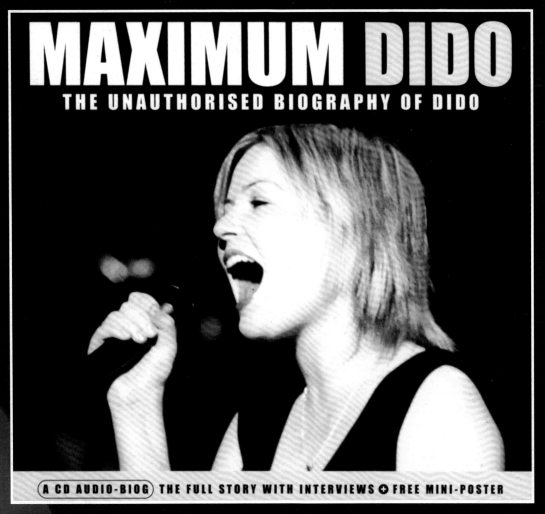

From the renowned Maximum series comes the complete
and unauthorised biography on Dido incorporating:

• Newly researched biographical information
• Exclusive comments and interview material from Dido herself
• Full-colour picture disc CD packaged with deluxe slipcase
• Free fold-out Dido poster
• Eight page illustrated booklet featuring rare photographs

Available from all good book and record shops or buy on-line at:

www.chromedreams.co.uk

Alternatively send a cheque or postal-order for £5.99 (£6.99 outside UK) to:
Chrome Dreams, PO BOX 230, New Malden, Surrey KT3 6YY, UK.

Catalogue Number: ABCD094

ISBN: 1 84240 153 X